HOPE ALT DELETE

NIKKI DUDLEY

NEWTON-LE-WILLOWS

Published in the United Kingdom in 2017
by The Knives Forks And Spoons Press,
51 Pipit Avenue,
Newton-le-Willows,
Merseyside,
WA12 9RG.

ISBN 978-1-909443-95-2

Copyright © Nikki Dudley, 2017.

The right of Nikki Dudley to be identified as the author of this work has been asserted by him in accordance with the Copyrights, Designs and Patents Act of 1988. All rights reserved. No part of this publication may be reproduced, stored in a retrieval system, transmitted in any form or by any means, electronic, photocopying, recording or otherwise, without prior permission of the publisher.

Acknowledgements:

Some of these poems first appeared in the *Walking Is Still Honest Press* and *Phase 47* (Ronin Press).

Thanks to the Fete des lumieres 2013 for the cover image.

Dedicated to the good people who are no longer with us and all the good people who still are.

Table of Contents

Ayuda	7
The day you died	9
The antidote	11
Hear you	12
Tunnels, dear	14
Two gather	15
future	16
Keats	18
Keep these pieces	19
Past written	21
Cellmate, Word	22
Everything	25
Stop the bus	26
The whirled	28
I route the end	29
Set the alarm	30
Crossed words	31
Hope	34

Die when I want to.	35
cost-benefit	36
Final fault	39
Eye saw you	40
Steadily metal	41
Back	42
Body of words	45
I.O.A	47
Notice. Period.	48
Ctrl+Z	50

Ayuda – if I calling you, *please*

me / answer someone
        something

Take notes: I is trying
grows into? A people a persons
      no childs, no more.

For example, in my case I carry
tols, *no*, tools
of land gu age – (quicker) – language
like sandwich.

Can you under-stand me?
Can you over-stand me?

Poe-hams are losing, poe hams are lost in ...
I going to be learning about
this, there there, <u>can you love</u>

me is difficult, I nose it. Don't need
to speak, no, I look it with
own –

Nikki Dudley

Fuck, lost in a word. How you
say lost
in a word?

Finding me is _____

                _____

                                  _____

                                          _____

The day you died

Wrote in it my diary a year in advance / red /
CAPS, screaming in a box.

We never spoke about it.

Everything rolled over me like I was land, unwilling
bystander in this cycle
of in-ev-it-a-ble steps / even if
we walked backwards, arms kept circling on your
aging face.

Didn't believe you were floating towards
      drowning, fighting your way in the dark

      (Did you remember who I was?)

because I told you I loved you ... hoped you heard ...
even when you were still

    --------------------fucking angry

Nikki Dudley

      Were you walking out on me or life?

The trees thrash like my mind thrashes thoughts of you, in between, memories jar me

(No one can see –

The darkness makes it fester, a disease that swarms me in dreams
                                 And will I wake up
                                 And will you stay with me
when the dreams throw me
              Out of time, my fingers
      stretched
          across the wood, shaking
     for the roots.

    Lost now.

Map is burning in the stream and I'm burning in the scream and I'm –
mid-sentence with

Hope Alt Delete

The antidote to language
is loneliness is loneliness why the masses don't deviate!
Let gold dust dis   app
ear in mud, lost property finds me. I am found material:
dad's nose/mum's eyes/ tendency towards
anger/stubbornness.

Keep together-now. Don't fix yourself.

Life happens and death happens / in a sent
hence don't cry over
accepting the antidote is a conspiracy to
a get out clause.

A politician watching the world:
"Did you pack hope???"
Spinning in the same direction those / who do not /
lost riots, changing nuffin to somefin.

Is loneliness the antidote to masses,
don't find material in the sand. Gold dust
happens (standing in the street) counting
lines, cracks, number plates and letters
spell thoughts.

If I save them / If I save coins
can eye spend a pen

Nikki Dudley

Hear you

as IF a tunnel, echo eco
ache-o, my heart.
Have you to think – keep in
the flesh, my bone don't

      find fun in

shatter ring and ear no
voice now.

Still got my lo
      ve
he don't fall
      part now cause
you believed in it despite what,
you kept me but forgot
you.

Tawking shit, I hear words like
too morrow, how long
here too? *Stay*.

Hope Alt Delete

Can't put worse in
words, never rights down, in the
night, inthenight, avalanche
your face
your face
the gauze skin, trumps
tears but I want
sleepless love, to no avail launches when
the words
                              run
definitely, run
not one
let her leave
to run

Nikki Dudley

Tunnels, dear

Tunnels talk,

a languid I can speak waiting for time

to collect me ten stops home.

Wait, the house

is gone but in dreams

home finds me between fires and failure and

I can't save them or him or you or

                                      I watch the world. Please

                let me

save you because I won't save

myself is a lost cause in compare

a sun, ask it not to eat us.

Like in my dreams, when I dream eye

roll over and try

        hold in (on)

Two gather

Only constraint / his time
rhyme something with ... lines or   lines.
Am I e-still a poet if miles to/from
The Start Line and I can't
          (remember where this all started?

No, me neither. Mark hers, I need mark hers.

The story is walking away from
      me,   or you,   or that girl,   who who
wrote
something about looking up, purr lease,
look up. There's nothing
we won't do two gather,
nothing we won't

/Someone/ told me a lie about the future
& I didn't believe a world.

Nikki Dudley

future is few all isle, bridges
are bridges if
they fall out, remember
I, nothing or will I
be a sum of things, or morse
code tap tap taptaptap tap tap

What you hear >whispers< enough
to start a wore / lies like lies
hung like empty frames and we're all
rested for crimes, guilty
until proven

Will the homes be crunched under
hors d'oeuvres, or fast-food fighting
(question answer question question question)
Where you putt them all, your course of
battleships, sunk
like dreams

Words change anything except
nothing, so
words changed
yes / no / under sided
not an option now
#grey 1 #grey 2

Hope Alt Delete

Your future few trial
unless

☐ deselect if you don't want to receive marketing
   from our partners and affiliates forever

Nikki Dudley

Keats

Don't wasta page,   see!

Call me summit I'm don't and eye
won't stand / I'll
forgive.

Words are nought in,
juss speakin' in diff-a-rant ways because
'istory and pride.

Will eyes love winta again?
Freezing is over they said,
com pain non ship broken they said - I
feel nothing ... So how can
I feel love.

PLEASE -

Tell me Keats new summit.

Hope Alt Delete

Keep these pieces

you can't make

it back? Scatter them

in the house like sticky leaves

on the autumn floor. Pages of a book

      nowhere definite.

They float around

      Disappear.

Give life to your laugh, flesh

to soft hands. I promise.

You linger

the jarring smell of cut grass, not obvious

but I stop - feel you.

Don't take these pie-sis, no matter

fly at half-mast to remember my name.

Stories / half-truths / words pick

through those threads to make you.

            (You won't ask me to take you home again.

                        You won't ask me to

                                take you home.)

Nikki Dudley

In the walls, the toaster when
still foggy with sleep. See you, even though you
lost the pieces somewhere behind
Is. Iris.

Past written

said about   home / the paper was
peeled / like a clementine I cudn't put right

the past written   down. It sounded
pause-able but no, (your love) is a plunge pool that I
can't love. A plunge pool and I
pot the white

in my heart. Objects may be   closer
than they   appear.

I know, know fool me -
a poker bluff in a ski mask but
itseemedlikeyou.

My eyes lost contact when
the camera refused / to be
eye for an I, it left (me (out (of

Nikki Dudley

Cellmate, Word

always in room(humming breathing farting).

On the run, you ratted me out, *then*
testified innocence. Do you   care? I wanted
but rolled over in bed / snored.

            Dreaming about stabbing me when I
    closed these Is……?

You you you vowels and consonants ganging
in the shower, crowding
hungry flies / looking for death. Your eyes
bulbous bulbous,
slits of light in the darkness all

At once (((What do you want from me? The bars?

Shrinking around [my heart],   *for my own*

protection?

Hope Alt Delete

You wrote on the walls and I left you alone.

Never spoke
about it, Word. Disguised yourself so
I could send   +*_&^
my family my friends, but you didn't
tell how you watched
minute, minute, second, first, zero how
you whispered to the prisoners and guards.

Come on, Word, why you coat my pillow
as my breathing   shallows and I drown.
Restless dreams, why you hang over
                        my bed - clouds

in the morning let the dreams mourn me
waiting for
sunlight, why you told me she might live
and told me she was dead, why you kept me
guarded between shelves cowering
beside lockers, why you taught
'I love you' but a million ways to lose. Tell me
you they he she we all want to hear

definition, synonyms, antonyms you're hiding
between your split ----- characters. Stop
talking, Word! This is the final final warning, before I
close my eyes
tight, block my ears
with glue, and tell
my brain not to think

but I will think. I hold tight when
all the lights
go / shivering in the dark, when
I open my eyes and soft shapes blurry light, when
my ears hum and
dull sounds ... I speculate, Word,
and hunt in the trenches for *h-o-m* - and
you pop up:

BOOM!

Everything

remember how
once i knew i was new but   not today.
Now i'm a shield of a per se, per-son-al-ly
I think
nothing will be better in the mourn innit.
Don't tell lies to ease ease ease me
like oil, i see them on the whites of
your eyes i can't trust (home)
enough things. Won't make this bet her a pound to see if
she will come back if she could
but nothing will be better.
You remember   how i knew her
and you did too you did but now the oil stains
 everything

Nikki Dudley

Stop the bus

stopping the bus, don't ask me
to lose you like the light in autumn, steadily and slowly
feeling each tone. Then. /a curtain/
The bus is going on and on and oh, don't…
1947 will never be the same without you if you
swallow our love because nothing else sticks
in your throat.

"No, no," you said. I laughed.

But the bus screeched at me when the phone rang rang / I ran
echoes of what we were, then, then and
the lies are coming to get us, a net that only one
escapes – "colours lie to me" – colours lie.

Don't ask me to stop, the bus will run over
everything (Don't ask,
keep the ghosts under
love and key. Love me under
lonely keys [will keep them out].

Throw yourself out of my scene? Throw your shell out to the fishes, to the fixes but/// the bug/// has wiped US clean, like polished nails, like polished nails we pierce
your skin. NO MORE.

The bus stopping but I
said no. I said keep your papery hand where I can see / keep your
papery heart where I can be. If my heart beats it beats me up, stop the bus, stop the bus. Stop. The. Bus. Stop.

Doors open and chest caves.
"My stop," you said did you?

Nikki Dudley

The whirled is dan generous
    – I could make a home but
home won't forgive.

Don't wannah loose threads, don't need
to re-invert – still
think about chile hood in the hood is
where I love.

Missing sum – think! Equations
are more easy, more easy
than pies and mash.

I root my words in cool her, can you
       still see
             me, por favor.

The streets. Streaks of light darkness,
bow tea full sky.

Don't you / Don't it
Forget the about

I route the end

closer to death than I ever been – chest
rising and falling /   slowly
                    choking ship.

A half-fault, half quiet cracks in me-dal
      tell me you'll hold on
oxygen   hold on too.

Fear ghostly
in the night, in day, in con – verse – actions.
That poison, I wrote

the end and it didn't stop
rotating hope a hired hit man / hope a matter of death.
Breathing in air / breathing out hope.
Useless flowers?
Do you want them cos I wrote the end, I rot it all down.
            And then I edit?

Set the alarm

1) I be right, there
2) Now words have turned to glass
3) LOST: Status
4) "You're too sensitive."
5) I said please, thank you
6) Now. Listen
7) Leave baggage at the banks
8) We are so incomplete, there is only hop
9) Keep the gloves ready
10) Pick a side and sick with it
11) I'll pick you up when you stand up
12) Ultimatum ...
13) Repetition repeats
14) Flesh loss
15) Speed dial 1: exit
16) At the end will be, past

Crossed words

Lost

    Lost

        Lost

a sea of disjunction.
Words butterflies we
cannot tame.

Glassy eyes swollen and
blind. Deceptively clear, clear
as rubble.

Wait. There. May. Be. Survivors.

Lost (we are
    misplaced

        absorbed

defeated, now now.

Nikki Dudley

Please do not write in the space below:

(for office purposes only)

Neck is impasse.

Let blood charge

toward the head and

      passage,

      passage,

      passage.

Can't write the way

out of floods. The belly drunk-

the holes, the body

the rising moat.

Words sterile needles,

hope in

to post message too the brain, two

the blood, to the   lost.

Hope Alt Delete

The announcement:

due to   circumstances
    not appearing   today
        apologizes
    disappointing   please
    rest   show

Talk in crosswords.
Put this together, meaning: 3 down, 4 letters:*adj*.
1 unable to find the way. **2** bewildered or helpless.
3 (*usu* + in) rapt or absorbed.

Hope

Learn

ing and develop

meant.

Hope is important, someone said?

awoke to lamplight, then

bulb shuddered and

nothing.

Time, hours, growing past,

cut myself out.

Hope is important, and eye sore

city swelling, water, waves

of memo reads:

waiting to rupture. STOP.

The flotsam never a survivor, in the mass

produced water, blood is saliva,

and hope is

sinking

re-surf-a-sin

hop

Die when I want to.

Robots with souls,
"You get drunk on the world ... Drunk
on the mystery of the world,"   What is the wind,
          what is it.
I would not, could not in a box. I could not,
would not, with a fox. *Jump start*,
with pro vitamin B5. Don't Ever Stop Observing
and Making Notes. Be a good communicator
verbally and in writing. It might even be a way
of giving the others hope.
     A GOOD IDEA IS BEST SHARED.
<u>LOST</u>: Grey + white pigeon, normal size,
a bit mangy looking. Does not have a name.
A single image is not splendour.

Nikki Dudley

cost-benefit

i promise to pay the bearer
on demand
        the sum of:
    a) two fountain pens
    b) several large dictionaries
    c) a peanut
    d) seven stolen sugar sachets
    e) a power cut

cannot save you if
you have choked on the word.

absence is a drug. The drug i saw
a bridge that goes

i thought of ... ALL
but a vowel.

i remembered.
                                            must load my
tongue
                                            with gold and read
                on a tightrope...

CAPITALISATION is a dictator.

i promise to pay the bearer
the sum of:
                    ON DEMAND!
i.o.u - 50 pence per vowel, 29 pence per full stop, 11.5
pence per image, 3 pence per
letters of peace are burnt in protest.

        However, the fish kept a strict diary of events.

take this down:
<u>alcohol is a tragic comedy</u>
(check accuracy)
                        have you seen the tariff for
wednesdays:

the sum of premise i demand

two pay.

my head is a balloon
to gush. road works are not
landmines and i'd like
to return
this reason: unwanted gift

IDON'TWANTTOBEJESUS

the bridge that goes
y*u y*u y*u y*u y*u.

nowhere i demand
                the bearer to pay
waste is the drug.
going once,
         going through THIS through

Final fault

Ground shakes for no one but
He is the definitive article / shhh / the forest
is fallen and the leaves
climb trees   waiting like a flood waits

Drowning is like washing, wash me
dry, wash my mouth with
paper before I say something I can't take

Cracks haunt me – see edges crack when
holding onto pieces of
love you all love you mostly

Tell me dreaming is half-mea-sure,
wonderland is hard-boiled (you) can't
escarpment
long way
 to fool.

Stay here ground me.

Nikki Dudley

Eye saw you

        in a dream

Tawking Smiling

like never left or right,

like you never dyed

                                        that room.

It was whiter than death when
you

                            leave me, alone,

                            and her, and them.

Eye sore   dreams but I didn't see
you know more about you than me know more about
death.

It was a dream it was please tell me it was
cause you ain't chalking
on that bed. Just keep moving
      outside the lines
               just moving
          are you still

Steadily metal

You trust wood?
It shuddered when I sawed it. Won't be
no alley bye, it ain't shiny
clean.

Wood don't met all,
no meet hall here. Find a friend you
won't flaunt, *oh wait*, a false friend...

Woodya trist metal in the ran???
Don't give a dam if it rains, give
a tonic I can trust.

No, steadily metal foe me, no wood
would you be? Met all metal is stronger
you say

Nikki Dudley

Back

Signs cracked eggshells, once promising life, benches black homeless,
street   lights   flicker   in
      embarrass   ment.

Chewing gun acne plague, puberty
is a trace of blood washed,
never reborn.

Went back.

         People ripples *drifting*
from centre of memory,   losing
definition, a photo graft
      reproduced, reproduced, reproduced
        image through water

Went back.

Houses cold, skin wrinkled, dolled in conversation.
Barricades, the trees / protestors waving, screaming

Hope Alt Delete

were forgotten
left
    leafless.

I went back, shops closetheirmouths, open them,
memories smeared on glass, ^cannot hide^.

      Back went I. When I went. I went when.
           When back went I.

Flats tower
over houses where
quiet park used to hibernate, where
trees laughed and dogs
crapped.

Back. The shit is a footprint,
into new luxury builds, into underground tubes like
vermin

The signs cracked eggshells, once promising life,
benches black
                          homeless,
  street   lights   flicker   houses cold,

Nikki Dudley

skin wrinkled.

Leafless shops closetheirmouths,

will soon curdle, hibernate, where the

plague, puberty

barricades.

Body of words

The occurrence of repetition   happens
everyday every day, repetition
occurs repetition is an every days occurrence.

Repeat rewind   fast-forward
stop poison poison stop
legs and arms and fingers and toes
arms and fingers and toes and legs
love what is take it back
a mirror a distortion.

Body will not forget
what you've done repeat repeat
rewind depression obsession
confession perhaps
sherbet lemon.

Tomorrow is the end of / immortality.
Tell a story until frothing at the ends
frothing at the eyes
talk talk talk froth until
we die my stomach

Nikki Dudley

is full of filling up teeming with
backwards back take me back words
force the holes in memory plug the holes in
sen tences.

Repeat rewind   fast-forward
stop stop please stop everything, repetition is
an every day occurrence everyday
repetition occurs the occurrence
of repetition ... everyday I love you
in the morning hate
the texture of glass cut my lips
you're a fixture I,   the body the body
won't forget press
reset.

I.O.A

Saw the sky

throwing light at the ground,

spiteful child. The trees

playing whispers, talking

behind my-

Won ted you.

Grass waved teasingly, remembered

drawing away and

took the page, tore it up for filling up with

U:I.O.An explanation.

Spaces prepare for expression,

you are my semi-colon

in a death order.

We are I's without dots.

Nikki Dudley

Notice. Period.

I saw I saw

the children the windows blown

the house spitting

the children circling

circling closer hunting

predators for bones

rubble cupped in palms bruised

bleeding bleeding bruised

Dust coughed /camouflaging before whispers hummed

out of ill silence and I saw I heard the dust

smelt sad

The children the children

should have fixed gaps

frowning ceiling the cracks

the cracks

bones cracked

Someone should

someone should

someone shroud

Hope Alt Delete

The children dust

palms of bones the bones of palms

and spat why

I saw why I saw

Nikki Dudley

Ctrl+Z

Shortcuts scar like sunlight
in the rain, in the reign I is no one
to change the
co-or-die-nuts am I?

Listen to the birds singeing in the morning
on my brain.
Happiness is hear happiness is
asleep next to me / don't fort get what
you has don't dell eat what you

I right the words because I can't
not, double negative makes a
pose ah tive.
Can't hide behind wars no more.

www.ingramcontent.com/pod-product-compliance
Lightning Source LLC
Chambersburg PA
CBHW031943070426
42450CB00006BA/865